Groundhog Day

by Lisa M. Herrington

Content Consultants

Nanci R. Vargus, Ed.D.
Professor Emeritus, University of Indianapolis

Carrie A. Bell, MST Visual Arts – All Grades
Julia A. Stark Elementary School, Stamford, Connecticut

Reading Consultant

Jeanne M. Clidas, Ph.D.
Reading Specialist

Children's Press®
An Imprint of Scholastic Inc.
New York Toronto London Auckland Sydney
Mexico City New Delhi Hong Kong
Danbury, Connecticut

Library of Congress Cataloging-in-Publication Data
Herrington, Lisa M.
  Groundhog day / by Lisa M. Herrington.
    pages cm. — (Rookie read-about holidays)
  Includes index.
  ISBN 978-0-531-27203-9 (library binding) — ISBN 978-0-531-27353-1 (pbk.)
  1. Groundhog Day—Juvenile literature. I. Title.
  GT4995.G6H47 2013
  394.261—dc23   2013014835

Produced by Spooky Cheetah Press

© 2014 by Scholastic Inc.

All rights reserved. Published in 2014 by Children's Press, an imprint of Scholastic Inc.

Printed in China 62

SCHOLASTIC, CHILDREN'S PRESS, ROOKIE READ-ABOUT®, and associated logos
are trademarks and/or registered trademarks of Scholastic Inc.

1 2 3 4 5 6 7 8 9 10 R 23 22 21 20 19 18 17 16 15 14

Photographs © 2014: Adam Chinitz: 28; Alamy Images/Michael Griffin: 31 top;
AP Images: 16, 31 bottom (Adrain Wyld/CP), 3 top, 15, 31 center top (Evgen
Kraws), 19 (Frank Gunn/CP), 24 (Laura Stoecker/Daily Herald), 7 (Ryan Taplin/CP),
23 (Todd Sumlin/The Charlotte Observer); Getty Images/Ray Coleman: 11, 30;
Louise Gardner: 4; Media Bakery: 12; Polaris Images/Shahar Azran: 20; Reuters/
Geoff Robins: 27; Superstock, Inc.: cover (F1 Online), 8, 31 center bottom (Juniors);
Thinkstock/Hemera: 3 bottom.

Table of Contents

FEBRUARY

SUNDAY	MONDAY	TUESDAY	WEDNESDAY	THURSDAY	FRIDAY	SATURDAY
						1
2	3	4	5	6	7	8
9	10	11	12	13	14	15
16	17	18	19	20	21	22
23	24	25	26	27	28	

4

Meet a Furry Forecaster!

Will the **groundhog** see its shadow this year? Most people cannot wait to find out on February 2nd, which is Groundhog Day!

FAST FACT!

Groundhogs are furry rodents like mice and squirrels. They are also called woodchucks.

5

Punxsutawney (PUNK-sit-taw-nee) Phil is one of the most famous groundhogs in the United States. He lives in Pennsylvania. Shubenacadie (SHOO-ben-ack-a-dee) Sam is one of Canada's most famous groundhogs. He lives in Nova Scotia.

This is a photo of Shubenacadie Sam.

A Groundhog's Tale

Here is how the Groundhog Day story goes. After **hibernating** for the winter, a groundhog comes out of its **burrow**. If it is cloudy, the groundhog will not see its shadow. It will stay outside. That means there will be an early spring.

These groundhogs are snuggled up in their winter burrow.

9

If the sun is shining, the groundhog will see its shadow. It will go back inside its burrow. People say that means there will be six more weeks of winter weather.

The groundhog is one of many animals that hibernate in winter.

Of course, a groundhog cannot really tell us when spring will begin! The holiday is just pretend.

By February, some people are tired of cold weather. They are ready for spring.

How It Began

For many years, people around the world relied on hibernating animals like groundhogs to predict the weather.

Mushko the groundhog lives in western Ukraine.

14

In the 1800s, people in the United States and Canada made Groundhog Day an official holiday. On Groundhog Day, people gather to learn the groundhog's prediction.

FAST FACT!

Most groundhogs have brown fur. But some have black fur or white fur.

17

Town **officials** dress up in fancy clothes. Early in the morning, the groundhog is "asked" for its prediction. An official puts his ear close to the groundhog. It looks like the groundhog is whispering a prediction.

Happy Groundhog Day!

There are lots of fun ways to celebrate Groundhog Day. People gather to watch the groundhog come out of its burrow. Others watch the news to find out if the groundhog has seen its shadow.

An official blows a fanfare trumpet as the crowd waits for groundhog Staten Island Chuck to come out.

21

In many places, people hold Groundhog Day ceremonies to celebrate.

Queen Charlotte predicts the weather in North Carolina.

Some people march in parades. Others gather to listen to music and celebrate with their neighbors.

In Woodstock, Illinois, people gather in the town square. They listen to music while they wait for the groundhog's prediction.

Some people even dress up in costumes to celebrate. How will *you* celebrate Groundhog Day?

These kids are wearing groundhog noses!

Make a Pop-Up Groundhog

What You'll Need

- Scissors
- Brown and green construction paper
- Glue
- Empty toilet paper roll

- Pencil
- Black marker
- Tape
- Craft stick

Directions

1. With an adult's help, cut enough green construction paper to cover the toilet paper roll. Glue the paper to the outside of the toilet paper roll.

2. Stand the toilet paper roll on the brown construction paper and use a pencil to trace around the base. Cut out the circle for the groundhog's head. Make sure it is small enough to fit in the toilet paper roll. Cut two smaller semicircles for the ears. Glue the ears onto the head.

3. Use the black marker to draw a face on your groundhog.

4. Tape the groundhog's head to the craft stick.

5. Push your groundhog up through its hole (the toilet paper roll). Do you see its shadow?

Show What You Know!

Spot the Shadow!

- Can you find the groundhog's shadow in the photo below?
- What causes the groundhog's shadow?
- What does it mean when a groundhog sees its shadow?

Think About It!

How do you think most people feel if they learn the groundhog sees its shadow? Why do you think they feel that way? How would *you* feel?

Glossary

burrow (BUR-oh): a hole or tunnel made by an animal

groundhog (GROUND-hog): a small, furry animal with large front teeth that lives in an underground home

hibernating (HYE-bur-nate-ing): sleeping during winter

officials (uh-FISH-uhls): people who hold important positions in organizations

Index

Facts for Now

Visit this Scholastic Web site for more information on Groundhog Day:
www.factsfornow.scholastic.com
Enter the keywords **Groundhog Day**

About the Author

Lisa M. Herrington is a freelance writer and editor. Every February 2, she eagerly awaits Punxsutawney Phil's prediction in hopes of an early spring. Lisa lives in Trumbull, Connecticut, with her husband, Ryan, and her daughter, Caroline.

32